AMAZING

BACON

RECIPES

Publications International, Ltd.

ISBN: 978-1-68022-266-1

Library of Congress Control Number: 2015951949

Manufactured in China.

8 7 6 5 4 3 2 1

Microwave Cooking: Microwave ovens vary in wattage. Use the cooking times as guidelines and check for doneness before adding more time.

TABLE OF CONTENTS

BACON BITES

BACON + ONION CHEESE BALL

MAKES 20 SERVINGS

1 package (8 ounces) cream cheese, softened

½ cup sour cream

½ cup bacon, crisp-cooked and crumbled

½ cup chopped green onions, plus additional for garnish

¼ cup crumbled blue cheese

Crackers and celery sticks (optional)

1 Beat cream cheese, sour cream, bacon, ½ cup green onions and blue cheese in large bowl until well blended. Shape mixture into a ball. Wrap in plastic wrap; refrigerate at least 1 hour.

2 Place cheese ball on serving plate. Garnish with additional green onions. Serve with crackers and celery, if desired.

CRUMB-TOPPED CLAMS

MAKES ABOUT 5 OR 6 SERVINGS

4 slices bacon

3 pounds live steamer or littleneck clams

⅓ cup finely chopped green onions

⅓ cup finely chopped fresh parsley

½ teaspoon grated lemon peel

2 tablespoons lemon juice

⅛ teaspoon hot pepper sauce

1 cup cracker crumbs

¼ cup grated Parmesan cheese

1 Cook bacon in large skillet over medium heat until crisp. Drain on paper towels. Crumble bacon. Discard all but 2 tablespoons drippings from skillet.

2 Tap clams and discard any that do not close. Scrub clams. Fill large saucepan with ½ inch of water; bring to a boil. Add clams; cover and cook 2 minutes or just until clams open. Transfer clams to large baking sheet. Discard top shells. Loosen clams from bottom of shells.

3 Preheat oven to 400°F. Pour reserved drippings into medium saucepan. Add green onions and parsley; cook and stir 1 minute or until tender. Remove from heat; add lemon peel, lemon juice and hot pepper sauce. Stir in cracker crumbs, Parmesan cheese and crumbled bacon.

4 Spoon crumb mixture over clams, pressing gently. Bake 5 minutes or until crumbs are golden brown.

CRUMB-TOPPED OYSTERS

Preheat oven to 400°F. Scrub 2 dozen oysters; remove top shell. Loosen oysters from bottom of shell; arrange on large baking sheet. Prepare crumb topping as directed and spoon over oysters, pressing gently. Bake 8 minutes or until oysters are just cooked and crumbs are golden brown.

SPICY DEVILED EGGS

MAKES 12 DEVILED EGGS

6 eggs

3 tablespoons whipping cream

1 green onion, finely chopped

1 tablespoon white wine vinegar

2 teaspoons Dijon mustard

½ teaspoon curry powder

½ teaspoon hot pepper sauce

3 tablespoons bacon, crisp-cooked and crumbled

1 tablespoon chopped fresh chives (optional)

1 Place eggs in small saucepan; cover with cold water. Bring to a boil over high heat. Cover and remove from heat; let stand 15 minutes. Drain and rinse under cold water. Peel eggs; cool completely.

2 Slice eggs in half lengthwise. Remove yolks to small bowl; set whites aside. Mash yolks with fork. Stir in cream, green onion, vinegar, mustard, curry powder and hot pepper sauce until blended.

3 Spoon or pipe egg yolk mixture into centers of egg whites. Arrange eggs on serving plate. Sprinkle bacon over eggs. Garnish with chives.

SMOKY BACON MUSHROOM TOASTS

MAKES 24 APPETIZERS

- 10 slices bacon
- 1 onion, diced
- 1 red bell pepper, diced
- 2 packages (8 ounces each) mushrooms, diced
- Salt and black pepper
- 24 (½-inch) toasted French bread slices
- Chopped fresh parsley

1 Cook bacon in large skillet over medium heat until crisp. Drain on paper towels. Discard all but 2 tablespoons drippings from skillet.

2 Add onion and bell pepper to skillet; cook and stir over medium-high heat 2 minutes or until tender. Add mushrooms; season with salt and black pepper. Cook and stir 8 to 10 minutes or until mushroom liquid is almost evaporated. Cool 5 minutes.

3 Crumble bacon. Spread 1½ tablespoons mushroom mixture on each bread slice. Sprinkle with crumbled bacon and parsley.

ROASTED RED POTATO BITES

MAKES 30 BITES

1½ pounds red potatoes (about 15 small)

 1 cup shredded Cheddar cheese (about 4 ounces)

 ½ cup HELLMANN'S® or BEST FOODS® Real Mayonnaise

 ½ cup sliced green onions

10 slices bacon, crisp-cooked and crumbled

 2 tablespoons chopped fresh basil leaves (optional)

1 Preheat oven to 400°F. On large baking sheet, arrange potatoes and bake 35 minutes or until tender. Let stand until cool enough to handle.

2 Cut each potato in half, then cut thin slice from bottom of each potato half. With small melon baller or spoon, scoop pulp from potatoes leaving ¼-inch shell. Place pulp in medium bowl; set shells aside.

3 Lightly mash pulp. Stir in remaining ingredients. Spoon or pipe potato filling into potato shells.

4 Arrange filled shells on baking sheet and broil 3 minutes or until golden and heated through.

GINGERED BBQ'D SHRIMP SKEWERS

MAKES 6 SERVINGS

Nonstick cooking spray

¼ cup barbecue sauce

¼ cup raspberry fruit spread

1 tablespoon grated fresh ginger

1½ tablespoons balsamic vinegar

⅛ teaspoon red pepper flakes

24 medium shrimp, peeled and deveined (with tails on)

4 bacon slices, each cut into 6 pieces

12 green onions, green part only, cut in half (24 pieces total)

1 can (8 ounces) pineapple chunks in juice, drained

12 (6-inch) bamboo skewers, soaked in water

1 Preheat grill to medium-high heat.

2 Coat cold grill rack with cooking spray and place over heat.

3 Combine barbecue sauce, fruit spread, grated ginger, vinegar and red pepper flakes in small bowl; whisk until well blended. Set aside.

4 Alternating shrimp, bacon, green onion and pineapple, thread skewers with 2 shrimp, 2 bacon pieces, 2 green onion pieces and 1 pineapple chunk per skewer.

5 Place half of sauce in separate bowl. Set aside.

6 Place skewers on grill, baste with remaining sauce and grill 3 minutes total or until shrimp are opaque in center, turning and basting frequently. Remove from heat, baste with reserved sauce.

PORKY PINWHEELS ▶

MAKES 24 PINWHEELS

1 sheet frozen puff pastry, thawed

1 egg white, beaten

8 slices bacon, crisp-cooked and crumbled

2 tablespoons packed brown sugar

¼ teaspoon ground red pepper

1 Place pastry on sheet of parchment paper. Brush with egg white.

2 Combine bacon, brown sugar and red pepper in small bowl. Sprinkle evenly over top of pastry; press lightly to adhere. Roll pastry jelly-roll style from long end. Wrap in parchment paper. Refrigerate 30 minutes.

3 Preheat oven to 400°F. Line baking sheet with parchment paper. Slice pastry into ½-inch-thick slices. Place 1 inch apart on prepared baking sheet.

4 Bake 10 minutes or until light golden brown. Remove to wire racks; cool completely.

BLT DIP

MAKES 3 CUPS

1 envelope LIPTON® RECIPE SECRETS® Onion Soup Mix*

1 cup HELLMANN'S® or BEST FOODS® Real Mayonnaise

1 container (8 ounces) sour cream

1 medium tomato, chopped (about 1 cup)

4 slices bacon, crisp-cooked and crumbled (about ⅓ cup)

Shredded lettuce (optional)

Also terrific with LIPTON® RECIPE SECRETS® Golden Onion Soup Mix.

1 Combine all ingredients except lettuce in medium bowl; chill, if desired.

2 Garnish with lettuce and serve with your favorite dippers.

BLT CUKES

MAKES 8 TO 10 PIECES

½ cup finely chopped lettuce

½ cup finely chopped baby spinach

3 slices bacon, crisp-cooked and crumbled

¼ cup finely diced tomato

1 tablespoon plus 1½ teaspoons mayonnaise

¼ teaspoon black pepper

⅛ teaspoon salt

1 large cucumber

Green onion or minced fresh parsley (optional)

1 Combine lettuce, spinach, bacon, tomato, mayonnaise, pepper and salt in medium bowl; mix well.

2 Peel cucumber; trim off ends and cut in half lengthwise. Use spoon to scoop out seeds; discard seeds.

3 Divide bacon mixture between cucumber halves, mounding in center. Garnish with green onions. Cut into 2-inch pieces.

TIP

Make these snacks when cucumbers are plentiful and large enough to easily hollow out with a spoon. Cucumbers are in season the months of May through August. These snacks can be made, covered and refrigerated up to 12 hours ahead of time.

TOMATO AND BACON QUESADILLAS

MAKES 8 SERVINGS

8 flour tortillas (8-inch soft taco size)

2 cups shredded Mexican cheese blend

1 can (14.5 ounces) HUNT'S® Petite Diced Tomatoes, drained

8 strips bacon, cooked, crumbled

½ cup loosely packed chopped fresh basil

WESSON® Vegetable Oil

Sour cream (optional)

LAYER over half of each tortilla: ¼ cup cheese, 2 tablespoons tomatoes, 1 tablespoon bacon and 1 tablespoon basil. Fold each tortilla over to form a half-circle.

COAT a large nonstick skillet or griddle lightly with oil. Cook each quesadilla, over medium-low heat, about 1½ minutes on each side until cheese is melted and the tortilla is lightly browned.

CUT each quesadilla into 4 wedges. Serve with sour cream, if desired.

BACON, BLUE CHEESE + RAMEN BITES

MAKES 8 SERVINGS (ABOUT 24 PIECES)

- 2 packages (3 ounces each) ramen noodles, any flavor, broken into 1-inch by 2-inch pieces*
- ¼ teaspoon black pepper, preferably coarsely ground
- ¼ cup roasted red peppers, chopped and patted dry on paper towels
- ¾ to 1 cup crumbled blue cheese
- 4 slices thick-cut bacon, cooked and crumbled
- 2 medium green onions, green part only, chopped

*Discard seasoning packets.

1 Preheat oven to 400°F. Line 13×9-inch baking pan with foil. Spray with nonstick cooking spray.

2 Place noodle pieces on prepared baking pan; sprinkle with black pepper. Top with red peppers, blue cheese, bacon and green onions.

3 Bake, uncovered, 12 to 15 minutes or until cheese bubbles.

NOTE

For a more pronounced flavor and more crunch, serve hot. For more blended flavor with a slight crunch, serve at room temperature.

HAWAIIAN PIZZA BITES

MAKES 15 TO 16 APPETIZERS

1 canister (13.9 oz.) refrigerated pizza crust dough

¾ cup pizza sauce

1½ cups shredded mozzarella cheese, divided

3 oz. sliced Canadian bacon, cut into small pieces

1 can (8 oz.) DOLE® Pineapple Tidbits or 1 can (20 oz.) DOLE® Pineapple Chunks, drained

Preheat oven to 400°F. Spray baking sheet with cooking spray.

Unroll dough onto lightly floured surface. Cut 15 to 16 circles with 3-inch cookie or biscuit cutter and place on baking sheet.

Bake 8 minutes. Remove from oven. Top crusts with pizza sauce, one-half cheese, Canadian bacon and pineapple tidbits. Top with remaining cheese.

Bake an additional 6 to 10 minutes or until crusts are golden brown.

BLT BISCUITS

MAKES 24 MINI SANDWICHES

2 cups all-purpose flour

2 teaspoons sugar

2 teaspoons baking powder

1 teaspoon black pepper

½ teaspoon baking soda

½ teaspoon salt

⅓ cup cold butter, cut into small pieces

1 cup (4 ounces) shredded Cheddar cheese

¾ cup buttermilk

½ cup mayonnaise

1 small head romaine lettuce, torn into small pieces

4 plum tomatoes, cut into ¼-inch slices

1 package (16 ounces) bacon slices, crisp-cooked and cut crosswise into 3 pieces

1 Preheat oven to 425°F. Line large baking sheets with parchment paper.

2 Combine flour, sugar, baking powder, pepper, baking soda and salt in large bowl. Cut in butter with pastry blender or two knives until mixture resembles coarse crumbs. Stir in cheese and buttermilk just until mixture forms dough.

3 Turn dough out onto lightly floured surface; knead gently several times. Pat into 8×6-inch rectangle (about ¾ inch thick). Cut dough into 24 squares with sharp knife; place on prepared baking sheets. Bake 10 to 12 minutes or until golden brown. Cool slightly on wire rack.

4 Split biscuits; spread each half lightly with mayonnaise. Layer each biscuit with lettuce, tomato and bacon.

TURKEY CLUB BISCUITS

Prepare BLT Biscuits as directed above, adding deli sliced turkey and avocado slices.

CHICKEN STUFFED JALAPEÑO WRAPS

MAKES 15 SERVINGS

- 1 pound boneless skinless chicken breasts, cut into strips
- 1 tablespoon minced garlic
- 1 tablespoon black pepper
- 2 teaspoons salt
- 1 teaspoon paprika
- 1 small onion, cut into strips
- 15 jalapeño peppers,* halved and seeded
- 1 pound bacon, halved crosswise
- Ranch salad dressing (optional)

Jalapeño peppers can sting and irritate the skin, so wear rubber gloves when handling peppers and do not touch your eyes.

1 Prepare grill for indirect cooking to medium heat.

2 Combine chicken, garlic, black pepper, salt and paprika in large resealable food storage bag; shake to coat.

3 Place 1 chicken strip and 1 onion strip in each jalapeño half. Wrap each jalapeño half with 1 piece bacon and secure with toothpicks.

4 Grill, uncovered, over indirect heat 20 minutes or until bacon is crisp cooked and chicken is cooked through, turning halfway through cooking time. Serve with ranch dressing, if desired.

SIZZLIN' STARTS

BACON + POTATO FRITTATA

MAKES 4 TO 6 SERVINGS

5 eggs

½ cup bacon, crisp-cooked and crumbled

¼ cup half-and-half or milk

⅛ teaspoon salt

⅛ teaspoon black pepper

3 tablespoons butter

2 cups frozen O'Brien hash brown potatoes
   with onions and peppers

1 Preheat broiler. Beat eggs in medium bowl. Add bacon,
half-and-half, salt and pepper; beat until well blended.

2 Melt butter in large ovenproof skillet over medium-high
heat. Add potatoes; cook and stir 4 minutes. Pour egg
mixture into skillet. Reduce heat to medium. Cover; cook
6 minutes or until eggs are set at edges (top will still be
wet).

3 Transfer skillet to broiler. Broil 4 inches from heat source
1 to 2 minutes or until top is golden brown and center
is set.

SERVING SUGGESTION

Top frittata with red bell pepper strips,
chopped chives and salsa.

CHEESY QUICHETTES

MAKES 12 QUICHETTES

12 slices bacon, crisp-cooked and chopped

6 eggs, beaten

¼ cup whole milk

1½ cups thawed frozen shredded hash brown potatoes, squeezed dry

¼ cup chopped fresh parsley

½ teaspoon salt

1½ cups (6 ounces) shredded Mexican cheese blend with jalapeño peppers

1 Preheat oven to 400°F. Lightly spray 12 standard (2½-inch) muffin cups with nonstick cooking spray.

2 Divide bacon evenly among prepared muffin cups. Beat eggs and milk in medium bowl. Add potatoes, parsley and salt; mix well. Spoon mixture evenly into muffin cups.

3 Bake 15 minutes or until knife inserted into centers comes out almost clean. Sprinkle evenly with cheese; let stand 3 minutes or until cheese is melted. (Egg mixture will continue to cook while standing.*) Gently run knife around edges and lift out with fork.

Standing also allows for easier removal of quichettes from pan.

BACON-CHEESE GRITS

MAKES 4 (¾-CUP) SERVINGS

2 cups milk

½ cup quick-cooking grits

1½ cups (6 ounces) shredded sharp Cheddar cheese *or* 6 slices American cheese, torn into bite-size pieces

2 tablespoons butter

1 teaspoon Worcestershire sauce

½ teaspoon salt

⅛ teaspoon ground red pepper (optional)

4 thick-cut slices bacon, crisp-cooked and chopped

1 Bring milk to a boil in large saucepan over medium-high heat. Slowly stir in grits. Return to a boil. Reduce heat; cover and simmer 5 minutes, stirring frequently.

2 Remove from heat. Stir in cheese, butter, Worcestershire sauce, salt and red pepper, if desired. Cover; let stand 2 minutes or until cheese is melted. Top each serving with bacon.

VARIATION

For a thinner consistency, add an additional ½ cup milk.

BACON AND EGGS BRUNCH CASSEROLE

MAKES 6 SERVINGS

1 tube (8 ounces) refrigerated crescent roll dough

6 eggs

½ cup milk

1 cup (4 ounces) SARGENTO® Traditional Cut Shredded Mild Cheddar Cheese

8 slices bacon, diced and cooked crisp

1 Spray 13×9-inch baking pan with nonstick cooking spray. Unroll dough and press into bottom of pan. Bake in preheated 350°F oven 10 minutes.

2 Beat together eggs and milk in medium bowl. Pour over partially baked dough. Sprinkle with cheese and bacon; return to oven and bake 25 minutes or until center is set.

BACON WAFFLES WITH MAPLE CREAM

MAKES 9 TO 10 WAFFLES

MAPLE CREAM

1 cup whipping cream

¼ cup maple syrup

WAFFLES

1 package (about 18 ounces)
butter-recipe yellow cake mix

1¼ cups buttermilk*

3 large eggs

½ cup (1 stick) butter, melted and cooled

¼ cup maple syrup

1 pound maple bacon, cooked and diced
(about 1¾ cups)**

*If buttermilk is unavailable, substitute
3½ teaspoons vinegar or lemon juice and
enough milk to equal 1¼ cups. Let stand
5 minutes.*

**Also delicious with applewood-smoked bacon.*

1 Preheat oven to 200°F. Place wire rack on baking
sheet; place in oven. Preheat waffle iron according to
manufacturer's directions. Spray cooking surface with
nonstick cooking spray.

2 Beat whipping cream and ¼ cup maple syrup in chilled
medium bowl with electric mixer at medium speed until
soft peaks form. Refrigerate until ready to serve.

3 Combine cake mix, buttermilk, eggs, butter and ¼ cup
maple syrup in large bowl. Add bacon; mix well. Spoon
batter by ½ cupfuls onto heated waffle iron (batter will be
thick). Cook 4 minutes or until steaming stops and waffles
are lightly browned. Remove to wire rack in oven to keep
warm. Repeat with remaining batter. Serve with chilled
maple cream.

BREAKFAST BISCUIT BAKE

MAKES 8 SERVINGS

8 ounces bacon, chopped

1 small onion, finely chopped

1 clove garlic, minced

¼ teaspoon red pepper flakes

5 eggs

¼ cup milk

½ cup (2 ounces) shredded white Cheddar cheese, divided

¼ teaspoon salt

⅛ teaspoon ground black pepper

1 package (16 ounces) refrigerated jumbo buttermilk biscuits (8 biscuits)

1 Preheat oven to 425°F. Cook bacon in large (10-inch) cast iron skillet until crisp. Remove bacon to paper towel-lined plate. Drain off and reserve drippings, leaving 1 tablespoon in skillet.

2 Add onion, garlic and red pepper flakes to skillet; cook and stir over medium heat 8 minutes or until onion is very soft. Set aside to cool slightly.

3 Whisk eggs, milk, ¼ cup cheese, salt and black pepper in medium bowl until well blended. Stir in onion mixture.

4 Wipe out any onion mixture remaining in skillet; grease with additional drippings, if necessary. Separate biscuits and arrange in single layer in bottom of skillet. (Bottom of skillet should be completely covered.) Pour egg mixture over biscuits; sprinkle with remaining ¼ cup cheese and cooked bacon.

5 Bake 25 minutes or until puffed and golden brown. Serve warm.

HASH BROWN CASSEROLE WITH BACON

MAKES 12 SERVINGS

1 package (32 ounces) refrigerated diced potatoes, thawed

1 container (16 ounces) sour cream

1 can (10¾ ounces) condensed cream of chicken soup, undiluted

1½ cups (6 ounces) shredded sharp Cheddar cheese

¾ cup thinly sliced green onions

4 slices bacon, crisp-cooked and crumbled

2 teaspoons hot pepper sauce

¼ teaspoon garlic salt

1 Preheat oven to 350°F. Spray 13×9-inch baking pan with nonstick cooking spray.

2 Combine potatoes, sour cream, soup, cheese, green onions, bacon, hot pepper sauce and garlic salt in large bowl. Spoon evenly into prepared pan.

3 Bake 55 to 60 minutes or until potatoes are tender and cooked through. Stir before serving.

BACON + EGG CUPS

MAKES 12 SERVINGS

12 slices bacon, crisp-cooked and cut crosswise into thirds

6 eggs

½ cup diced green and red bell pepper

½ cup (2 ounces) shredded pepper jack cheese

½ cup half-and-half

¼ teaspoon salt

¼ teaspoon black pepper

1 Preheat oven to 350°F. Lightly spray 12 standard (2½-inch) muffin cups with nonstick cooking spray.

2 Place 3 bacon slices in each prepared muffin cup, overlapping in bottom. Beat eggs, bell pepper, cheese, half-and-half, salt and black pepper in medium bowl until well blended. Fill each muffin cup with ¼ cup egg mixture.

3 Bake 20 to 25 minutes or until eggs are set in center. Run knife around edge of each cup before removing from pan.

TIP

To save time, look for mixed diced bell peppers in the produce section of the grocery store.

WHOLE WHEAT BACON AND EGG TACOS

MAKES 6 TACOS

1 tablespoon butter

10 eggs, lightly beaten

½ cup milk

½ teaspoon salt

½ teaspoon black pepper

6 slices bacon

6 (8-inch) ORTEGA® Whole Wheat Soft Tortillas

1 cup ORTEGA® Salsa, any variety

½ cup (2 ounces) shredded Cheddar cheese

MELT butter in medium skillet over medium heat. Combine eggs with milk, salt and pepper; pour into skillet. Scramble eggs to desired doneness. Remove from heat; set aside.

FRY bacon in medium skillet over medium heat. Remove from skillet; drain on paper towels.

HEAT dry skillet over medium heat. Place tortillas in skillet 1 to 2 minutes or until warm and pliable.

DIVIDE eggs evenly among tortillas, placing down center of each tortilla. Add 1 slice bacon and salsa; sprinkle evenly with Cheddar cheese. Fold in half. Serve immediately.

TIPS

Replace the bacon with sausage links or slices of deli ham for different variations of the recipe.

To heat tortillas in a microwave oven, wrap tortillas with a clean, lightly moistened cloth or paper towels. Microwave on HIGH (100% power) 1 minute or until hot and pliable.

STUFFED MEXICAN BREAKFAST POTATOES

MAKES 8 SERVINGS

4 russet potatoes

1 can (4 ounces) ORTEGA® Diced Jalapeños

1 cup ORTEGA® Salsa, any variety

4 eggs

1 can (15 ounces) ORTEGA® Black Beans, rinsed, drained

4 strips cooked bacon, crumbled

2 cups (8 ounces) shredded Cheddar cheese

Additional ORTEGA® salsa

PREHEAT oven to 350°F.

BAKE potatoes 1 hour or until done. Allow to cool before handling.

CUT in half; scoop out centers into medium bowl, leaving ⅛-inch shells. Add jalapeños to potatoes; mash well. Add 1 cup salsa; mix well.

COAT medium nonstick skillet with nonstick cooking spray. Scramble eggs to desired consistency over medium heat.

DIVIDE potato mixture evenly among potato skins. Top evenly with eggs, black beans, bacon and cheese.

BAKE 10 minutes or until the cheese is melted. Serve with additional salsa.

CARAMELIZED BACON

MAKES 6 SERVINGS

12 slices (about 12 ounces) applewood-smoked bacon

½ cup packed brown sugar

2 tablespoons water

¼ to ½ teaspoon ground red pepper

1 Preheat oven to 375°F. Line 15×10-inch jelly-roll pan with heavy-duty foil. Spray wire rack with nonstick cooking spray; place in prepared pan.

2 Cut bacon in half crosswise, if desired; arrange in single layer on prepared wire rack. Combine brown sugar, water and red pepper in small bowl; mix well. Brush generously over bacon.

3 Bake 20 to 25 minutes or until bacon is well browned. Immediately remove to serving platter; cool completely.

NOTE

Bacon can be prepared up to three days ahead and stored in the refrigerator between sheets of waxed paper in a large resealable food storage bag. Let stand at room temperature at least 30 minutes before serving.

MAPLE, BACON + RASPBERRY PANCAKE

MAKES 8 SERVINGS

5 slices bacon

2 cups pancake mix

1 cup water

½ cup maple syrup, plus additional for serving

1 cup fresh raspberries

3 tablespoons chopped pecans, toasted*

To toast pecans, spread in single layer in heavy skillet. Cook over medium heat 1 to 2 minutes or until nuts are lightly browned, stirring frequently.

1 Heat large skillet over medium heat. Add bacon; cook and stir until crisp. Remove to paper towel-lined plate using slotted spoon; crumble.

2 Brush inside of 5-quart slow cooker with 1 to 2 tablespoons bacon fat from skillet. Combine pancake mix, water and ½ cup syrup in large bowl; stir to blend. Pour half of batter into slow cooker; top with half of raspberries, half of bacon and half of pecans. Pour remaining half of batter over top; sprinkle with remaining raspberries, bacon and pecans.

3 Cover; cook on HIGH 1½ to 2 hours or until pancake has risen and is cooked through. Turn off heat. Let stand, uncovered, 10 to 15 minutes. Remove pancake from slow cooker; cut into eight pieces. Serve with additional syrup.

ALL WRAPPED UP

CHICKEN TENDERS IN BACON BLANKETS

MAKES 4 SERVINGS

¼ cup Dijon mustard

¼ cup maple syrup

¼ teaspoon chili powder

4 chicken breast tenders, cut in half lengthwise (about 12 ounces)

8 slices bacon

1 Preheat broiler. Combine mustard, maple syrup and chili powder in medium bowl. Reserve half of mustard mixture. Brush each chicken tender with remaining mustard mixture. Wrap 1 bacon slice around each chicken tender.

2 Place chicken tenders, bacon ends down, on rack of broiler pan. Broil 5 inches from heat 4 to 5 minutes on each side or until bacon is crisp and chicken is no longer pink in center. Serve with reserved mustard mixture for dipping.

BACON-WRAPPED APRICOTS

MAKES 14 SERVINGS

14 slices bacon, cut in half crosswise

¼ cup packed brown sugar

½ teaspoon black pepper

28 Mediterranean dried apricots* (one 7-ounce package)

14 water chestnuts, drained and cut in half crosswise

Mediterranean dried apricots are plump, pitted and whole apricots, available in the dried fruit section of most supermarkets.

1 Preheat oven to 425°F. Line shallow baking pan or baking sheet with parchment paper.

2 Sprinkle bacon with brown sugar and pepper, pressing to adhere. Fold apricot around water chestnut half. Wrap with half slice bacon; secure with toothpick.

3 Arrange apricots in prepared pan, spacing at least 1 inch apart. Bake 20 minutes or until bacon is cooked through, turning once.

RANCH-STYLE SHRIMP AND BACON APPETIZERS

MAKES 10 SHRIMP SKEWERS

Ranch-Style Barbecue Sauce (page 53)

30 large peeled, deveined shrimp

½ pound thick-cut bacon

10 wooden skewers*

To prevent wooden skewers from burning while grilling or broiling, soak in water about 10 minutes before using.

1 Prepare Ranch-Style Barbecue Sauce.

2 Wrap each shrimp with ½ bacon strip. Thread 3 wrapped shrimp onto each wooden skewer.

3 Grill or broil shrimp skewers until bacon is cooked and shrimp is no longer translucent, but has turned pink. Baste with Ranch-Style Barbecue Sauce. Return to heat to warm sauce. Serve with additional Ranch-Style Barbecue Sauce, if desired.

RANCH-STYLE BARBECUE SAUCE

MAKES 3 CUPS SAUCE

- ¼ cup vegetable or olive oil
- ½ cup minced onion
- 2 cloves garlic, minced
- 2 tablespoons lemon juice
- 1 tablespoon ground black pepper
- 1 teaspoon dry mustard
- 1 teaspoon paprika
- ½ teaspoon salt
- ½ teaspoon hot pepper sauce
- 1½ cups ketchup
- 1 cup HEATH® BITS 'O BRICKLE® Toffee Bits
- ¼ cup cider vinegar
- 3 tablespoons sugar
- 1½ tablespoons HERSHEY'®S Cocoa

1 Heat oil in large saucepan over medium heat; add onion and garlic. Cook until tender. Stir in lemon juice, black pepper, mustard, paprika, salt and hot pepper sauce. Simmer for 5 minutes; reduce heat.

2 Stir in ketchup, toffee bits, vinegar, sugar and cocoa. Simmer 15 minutes. Refrigerate leftovers.

CRISPY BACON STICKS

MAKES 10 STICKS

¾ cup (1½ ounces) grated Wisconsin Parmesan cheese, divided

5 slices bacon, halved lengthwise

10 breadsticks

MICROWAVE DIRECTIONS

Spread ¼ cup cheese on plate. Press one side of bacon into cheese; wrap diagonally around breadstick with cheese-coated side toward stick. Place on paper plate or microwave-safe baking sheet lined with paper towels. Repeat with remaining bacon halves, cheese and breadsticks. Microwave on HIGH 4 to 6 minutes or until bacon is cooked, checking for doneness after 4 minutes. Roll again in remaining ¼ cup Parmesan cheese. Serve warm.

WISCONSIN MILK MARKETING BOARD

BACON-WRAPPED BBQ CHICKEN

MAKES 4 SERVINGS

8 chicken tenders (about 1 pound)

½ teaspoon paprika or ground cumin (optional)

8 slices bacon

½ cup barbecue sauce

1 Preheat broiler. Line broiler pan with foil.

2 Sprinkle chicken tenders with paprika, if desired. Wrap each chicken tender with 1 slice of bacon in spiral pattern; place on prepared pan.

3 Broil chicken 4 minutes. Turn and broil 2 minutes. Brush with ¼ cup barbecue sauce; broil 2 minutes. Turn and brush with remaining ¼ cup barbecue sauce; broil 2 minutes or until chicken is no longer pink in center.

APRICOT BBQ GLAZED SHRIMP + BACON

MAKES 36 APPETIZERS

1 can (8 ounces) sliced water chestnuts, drained

36 medium raw shrimp, peeled and deveined (about 1¼ pounds)

9 slices bacon, each cut into 4 pieces

⅓ cup apricot fruit spread

⅓ cup barbecue sauce

1 tablespoon grated fresh ginger

1 tablespoon cider vinegar

⅛ teaspoon red pepper flakes

1 Preheat broiler. Place 1 water chestnut slice on top of each shrimp. Wrap 1 piece of bacon around shrimp and water chestnut; secure with toothpick. Repeat with remaining water chestnuts, shrimp and bacon.

2 Line broiler pan with foil; insert broiler rack. Coat broiler rack with nonstick cooking spray. Place shrimp on rack.

3 Combine fruit spread, barbecue sauce, ginger, vinegar and red pepper flakes in small bowl. Brush sauce evenly over appetizers. Broil 2 minutes; turn. Baste and broil 2 minutes; turn again. Baste and broil 1 minute or until bacon is browned.

BACON-WRAPPED FINGERLING POTATOES WITH THYME

MAKES 4 TO 6 SERVINGS

1 pound fingerling potatoes

2 tablespoons olive oil

1 tablespoon minced fresh thyme, plus additional for garnish

½ teaspoon black pepper

¼ teaspoon paprika

½ pound bacon slices

¼ cup chicken broth

SLOW COOKER DIRECTIONS

1 Toss potatoes with oil, 1 tablespoon thyme, pepper and paprika in large bowl.

2 Cut each bacon slice in half lengthwise; wrap half slice of bacon tightly around each potato.

3 Heat large skillet over medium heat; add potatoes. Reduce heat to medium-low; cook until lightly browned and bacon has tightened around potatoes.

4 Place potatoes in 4½-quart slow cooker. Add broth. Cover; cook on HIGH 3 hours. Garnish with additional thyme.

TIP

This appetizer can be made even more eye-catching with rare varieties of potatoes. Many interesting types of small potatoes can be found at farmers' markets. Purple potatoes, about the size of fingerling potatoes, can add some more color to this dish.

BRANDY-SOAKED SCALLOPS

MAKES 8 SERVINGS

1 pound bacon, cut in half crosswise

2 pounds small sea scallops

½ cup brandy

⅓ cup olive oil

2 tablespoons chopped fresh parsley

1 clove garlic, minced

1 teaspoon black pepper

½ teaspoon salt

½ teaspoon onion powder

1 Wrap 1 piece of bacon around each scallop; secure with toothpick, if necessary. Place wrapped scallops in 13×9-inch baking dish.

2 Combine brandy, oil, parsley, garlic, pepper, salt and onion powder in small bowl; mix well. Pour mixture over scallops; cover and marinate in refrigerator at least 4 hours.

3 Remove scallops from marinade; discard marinade. Arrange scallops on rack of broiler pan. Broil 4 inches from heat 7 to 10 minutes or until bacon is browned. Turn; broil 5 minutes or until scallops are opaque. Remove toothpicks.

BACON-WRAPPED STUFFED JALAPEÑOS

MAKES 24 APPETIZERS

1 package (8 ounces) cream cheese

1 cup (4 ounces) finely shredded Cheddar cheese

1 packet (1.25 ounces) ORTEGA® Taco Seasoning Mix

12 large jalapeño peppers*

12 slices bacon, cut in half

Jalapeño peppers can sting and irritate the skin, so wear rubber gloves when handling peppers and do not touch your eyes.

PREHEAT oven to 375°F. Place baking rack over baking sheet; set aside.

PLACE cream cheese in small microwavable bowl. Microwave on HIGH 1 minute; stir. If necessary, heat in 15-second intervals until cream cheese is softened. Stir in Cheddar cheese and seasoning mix; set aside.

CUT each jalapeño in half vertically; remove seeds and membrane. Fill with cream cheese mixture. Wrap bacon slices around jalapeños; secure with toothpick. Place on prepared rack.

BAKE 25 minutes. Turn on broiler; place baking sheet and rack 4 to 5 inches from heat. Broil jalapeños 3 to 4 minutes or just until bacon is lightly browned. Serve immediately.

TIP

If jalapeño peppers are too hot for you, prepare these appetizers using small sweet peppers cut in half.

BACON-WRAPPED BREADSTICKS

MAKES 16 BREADSTICKS

8 slices bacon

16 garlic-flavored breadsticks (about 8 inches long)

¾ cup grated Parmesan cheese

2 tablespoons chopped fresh parsley (optional)

MICROWAVE DIRECTIONS

1 Cut bacon slices in half lengthwise. Wrap half slice of bacon diagonally around each breadstick. Combine Parmesan cheese and parsley, if desired, in shallow dish; set aside.

2 Place 4 breadsticks on double layer of paper towels in microwave oven. Microwave on HIGH 2 to 3 minutes or until bacon is cooked through. Immediately roll breadsticks in Parmesan mixture to coat. Repeat with remaining breadsticks.

BACON-WRAPPED TERIYAKI SHRIMP

MAKES 4 TO 5 SERVINGS

1 pound large raw shrimp, peeled and deveined (with tails on)

¼ cup teriyaki marinade

11 to 12 slices bacon

1 Preheat oven to 425°F. Line shallow baking pan with foil. Set aside.

2 Place shrimp in large resealable food storage bag. Add teriyaki marinade; seal bag. Turn bag to coat shrimp. Marinate in refrigerator 15 to 20 minutes.

3 Meanwhile, separate bacon slices and cut in half crosswise.

4 Remove shrimp from bag, reserving marinade. Wrap each shrimp with 1 piece of bacon. Place shrimp on prepared baking pan; brush bacon with some of reserved marinade. Bake 15 minutes or until shrimp are pink and opaque.

TIP

Do not use thick-cut bacon for this recipe, because the bacon will not be completely cooked when the shrimp are done.

SOUPS, SALADS + SIDES

ANGRY CLAM CHOWDER

MAKES 8 SERVINGS

3 bacon slices, diced

1 onion, diced (about 1 cup)

1 stalk celery, diced

2 carrots, peeled and diced (about 1 cup)

1 can (7 ounces) ORTEGA® Diced Jalapeños

1 jar (16 ounces) ORTEGA® Salsa, Medium

1 pound minced clams

2 cups red potatoes, diced

BROWN bacon in large stockpot over medium heat 4 minutes or until crispy. Push bacon aside; add onion, celery, carrots and jalapeños. Toss to coat with bacon and continue to cook 5 minutes or until vegetables become wilted.

ADD salsa, 2 salsa jars of water and clams. Stir to combine; add potatoes. Reduce heat to low; cover and cook 15 minutes until the potatoes are cooked and soup is slightly thickened.

TIP

For an even spicier chowder, add ORTEGA® Taco Sauce. For more texture, sprinkle with crushed ORTEGA® Corn Taco Shells.

GRILLED SHRIMP SALAD WITH HOT BACON VINAIGRETTE

MAKES 4 SERVINGS

- 4 strips bacon, chopped
- ½ cup prepared Italian or vinaigrette salad dressing
- ⅓ cup FRENCH'S® Honey Dijon Mustard or FRENCH'S® Honey Mustard
- 2 tablespoons water
- 8 cups mixed salad greens
- 1 cup diced yellow bell peppers
- 1 cup halved cherry tomatoes
- ½ cup pine nuts
- 1 pound jumbo or extra large shrimp, shelled, with tails left on

1 Cook bacon until crisp in medium skillet. Whisk in salad dressing, mustard and water; keep warm over very low heat.

2 Place salad greens, bell peppers, tomatoes and pine nuts in large bowl; toss. Arrange on salad plates.

3 Cook shrimp in an electric grill pan or barbecue grill 3 minutes or until pink. Arrange on salads, dividing evenly. Serve with dressing.

BACON-JALAPEÑO CORNBREAD

MAKES 9 TO 12 SERVINGS

4 slices bacon

¼ cup minced green onions

2 jalapeño peppers,* stemmed, seeded and minced

1 cup all-purpose flour

1 cup yellow cornmeal

2½ teaspoons baking powder

¾ teaspoon salt

½ teaspoon baking soda

1 egg

¾ cup plain yogurt

¾ cup milk

¼ cup (½ stick) butter, melted

½ cup (2 ounces) shredded Cheddar cheese

Jalapeño peppers can sting and irritate the skin, so wear rubber gloves when handling peppers and do not touch your eyes.

1 Preheat oven to 400°F.

2 Cook bacon in large skillet over medium heat until crisp. Drain on paper towels. Pour 2 tablespoons drippings into 9-inch square baking pan or cast iron skillet.

3 Crumble bacon into small bowl; add green onions and jalapeño peppers. Combine flour, cornmeal, baking powder, salt and baking soda in large bowl.

4 Beat egg slightly in medium bowl; add yogurt and whisk until smooth. Whisk in milk and butter. Pour mixture into dry ingredients; stir just until moistened. Stir in bacon mixture. Pour into prepared pan; sprinkle with cheese.

5 Bake 20 to 25 minutes or until wooden toothpick inserted into center comes out clean. Cut into squares or wedges.

SANTA FE BBQ RANCH SALAD

MAKES 4 SERVINGS

1 cup *Cattlemen's*® Golden Honey Barbecue Sauce, divided

½ cup ranch salad dressing

1 pound boneless, skinless chicken

12 cups washed and torn Romaine lettuce

1 small red onion, thinly sliced

1 small ripe avocado, diced ½-inch

4 ripe plum tomatoes, sliced

2 cups shredded Monterey Jack cheese

½ cup cooked, crumbled bacon

1 Prepare BBQ Ranch Dressing: Combine ½ cup barbecue sauce and salad dressing in small bowl; reserve.

2 Grill or broil chicken over medium-high heat 10 minutes until no longer pink in center. Cut into strips and toss with remaining ½ cup barbecue sauce.

3 Toss lettuce, onion, avocado, tomatoes, cheese and bacon in large bowl. Portion on salad plates, dividing evenly. Top with chicken and serve with BBQ Ranch Dressing.

TIP

Serve *Cattlemen's*® Golden Honey Barbecue Sauce as a dipping sauce with chicken nuggets or seafood kabobs.

BACON-ROASTED BRUSSELS SPROUTS

MAKES 4 SERVINGS

1 pound Brussels sprouts

3 slices bacon, cut into ½-inch pieces

2 teaspoons packed brown sugar

Salt and black pepper

1 Preheat oven to 400°F. Trim ends from Brussels sprouts; cut in half lengthwise.

2 Combine Brussels sprouts, bacon and brown sugar in glass baking dish.

3 Roast 25 to 30 minutes or until golden brown, stirring once. Season with salt and pepper.

LEEK + POTATO SOUP

MAKES 4 TO 6 SERVINGS

5 cups shredded frozen hash brown potatoes

3 leeks, cut into ¾-inch pieces

1 can (10¾ ounces) condensed cream of potato soup, undiluted

1 can (about 14 ounces) chicken broth

2 stalks celery, sliced

1 can (5 ounces) evaporated milk

6 slices bacon, crisp-cooked, chopped and divided

½ cup sour cream

SLOW COOKER DIRECTIONS

1 Combine potatoes, leeks, soup, broth, celery, evaporated milk and all but 2 tablespoons bacon in slow cooker. Cover; cook on LOW 6 to 7 hours.

2 Stir in sour cream. Sprinkle with reserved bacon.

BROCCOLI SLAW

MAKES 6 TO 8 SERVINGS

- 1 package (12 ounces) broccoli slaw
- 6 slices bacon, crisp-cooked and crumbled
- ½ small red onion, chopped
- 1 package (3 ounces) ramen noodles, any flavor, crumbled and divided*
- ¼ cup roasted salted sunflower seeds
- 1 cup mayonnaise
- 2 tablespoons sugar
- 2 tablespoons cider vinegar
- ¼ teaspoon black pepper

Discard seasoning packet.

1 Combine broccoli slaw, bacon, onion, half of noodles and sunflower seeds in large bowl.

2 Whisk mayonnaise, sugar, vinegar and pepper in small bowl. Pour over slaw mixture; stir to combine. Garnish with remaining noodles. Serve immediately.

TIP

Any chopped nuts, such as peanuts or almonds, can be substituted for the sunflower seeds.

BAKED POTATO SOUP

MAKES 8 SERVINGS

3 cans (10¾ ounces each) condensed cream of
   mushroom soup

4 cups milk

3 cups diced peeled baked potatoes

½ cup cooked crumbled bacon

1 tablespoon fresh thyme leaves *or* 1 teaspoon dried
   thyme leaves

Sour cream and shredded Cheddar cheese

1½ cups FRENCH'S® French Fried Onions

1 Combine soup and milk in large saucepan until blended.
Stir in potatoes, bacon and thyme. Cook over medium
heat about 10 to 15 minutes or until heated through,
stirring frequently. Season to taste with salt and pepper.

2 Ladle soup into serving bowls. Top each serving with sour
cream, cheese and 3 tablespoons French Fried Onions.

COBB SALAD

MAKES 4 SERVINGS

1 package (10 ounces) torn mixed salad greens *or* 8 cups torn romaine lettuce

6 ounces deli chicken, turkey or smoked turkey breast, diced

1 large tomato, seeded and chopped

⅓ cup bacon, crisp-cooked and crumbled

1 large ripe avocado, diced

   Crumbled blue cheese

   Prepared blue cheese or Caesar salad dressing

1 Place salad greens in large serving bowl. Arrange chicken, tomato, bacon and avocado in rows.

2 Sprinkle with blue cheese. Serve with dressing.

SERVING SUGGESTION

Serve with warm French or Italian rolls.

LOADED GRILLED POTATO PACKET

MAKES 4 TO 6 SERVINGS

REYNOLDS WRAP® Non-Stick Foil

4 medium potatoes, cut into ½-inch cubes

1 large onion, diced

2 tablespoons olive oil

4 slices bacon, cooked and crumbled

2 teaspoons seasoned salt

1 tablespoon chopped fresh chives

1 cup shredded Cheddar cheese

Sour cream (optional)

PREHEAT grill to medium-high or oven to 450°F.

CENTER potatoes and onion on sheet of REYNOLDS WRAP® Non-Stick Foil with non-stick (dull) side toward food. Drizzle with olive oil. Sprinkle with crumbled bacon, seasoned salt, chives and cheese.

BRING up foil sides. Double fold top and ends to seal, making one large foil packet, leaving room for heat circulation inside.

GRILL 18 to 20 minutes in covered grill **OR BAKE** 30 to 35 minutes on a cookie sheet in oven. If desired, serve with sour cream.

SOUPS, SALADS + SIDES

KETTLE-COOKED BAKED BEANS WITH SMOKED SAUSAGE

MAKES 8 SERVINGS

- 1 package (2.1 ounces) fully cooked bacon, chopped
- 1 pound smoked sausage, sliced diagonally
- 1 medium onion, chopped (about ½ cup)
- 2 cans (31 ounces each) VAN CAMP'S® Pork and Beans
- 1 can (6 ounces) HUNT'S® Tomato Paste
- ½ cup HUNT'S® Ketchup
- ¼ cup packed brown sugar
- 2 tablespoons GULDEN'S® Spicy Brown Mustard

SLOW COOKER DIRECTIONS

1 Combine bacon, sausage, onion, beans, tomato paste, ketchup, brown sugar and mustard in slow cooker.

2 Cook on LOW setting for 4 to 6 hours or on HIGH setting for 2 to 3 hours. Stir before serving.

BLT CHICKEN SALAD FOR TWO

MAKES 2 SERVINGS

- 2 boneless skinless chicken breasts
- ¼ cup mayonnaise or salad dressing, plus additional for topping
- ½ teaspoon black pepper
- 4 large lettuce leaves
- 1 large tomato, seeded and diced
- 3 slices bacon, crisp-cooked and crumbled
- 1 hard-cooked egg, chopped

1 Prepare grill for direct cooking.

2 Brush chicken with ¼ cup mayonnaise; sprinkle with pepper. Grill over medium heat 5 to 7 minutes per side or until no longer pink in center. Cool slightly; cut into thin strips.

3 Arrange lettuce on serving plates. Top with chicken, tomato, bacon and egg. Spoon additional mayonnaise over top, if desired.

BLACK BEAN AND BACON SOUP

MAKES 6 TO 8 SERVINGS

5 strips bacon, sliced

1 medium onion, diced

2 tablespoons ORTEGA® Fire-Roasted Diced Green Chiles

2 cans (15 ounces each) ORTEGA® Black Beans, undrained

4 cups chicken broth

½ cup ORTEGA® Taco Sauce, any variety

½ cup sour cream

4 ORTEGA® Yellow Corn Taco Shells, crumbled

COOK bacon in large pot over medium heat 5 minutes or until crisp. Add onion and chiles. Cook 5 minutes or until onion begins to brown. Stir in beans, broth and taco sauce. Bring to a boil. Reduce heat to low. Simmer 20 minutes.

PURÉE half of soup in food processor until smooth (or use immersion blender in pot). Return puréed soup to pot and stir to combine. Serve with dollop of sour cream and crumbled taco shells.

NOTE

For a less chunky soup, purée the entire batch and cook an additional 15 minutes.

TWO-TONED STUFFED POTATOES

MAKES 6 SERVINGS

3 large baking potatoes (12 ounces each)

2 large sweet potatoes (12 ounces each), dark flesh preferred

3 slices thick-cut bacon, cut in half crosswise diagonally

2 cups chopped onions

⅔ cup buttermilk

¼ cup (½ stick) butter, cut into small pieces

¾ teaspoon salt, divided

1 Preheat oven to 450°F. Pierce potatoes with fork in several places. Bake directly on rack 45 minutes or until fork-tender. Let potatoes stand until cool enough to handle. *Reduce oven temperature to 350°F.*

2 Meanwhile, cook bacon in medium skillet over medium-high heat 6 to 8 minutes or until crisp. Remove from heat; transfer bacon to paper towels.

3 Add onions to drippings in skillet; cook 12 minutes over medium-high heat or until golden brown. Remove onions from skillet; set aside. Stir buttermilk into skillet, scraping up any browned bits from bottom of pan. Add butter; stir until melted.

4 Cut baking potatoes in half lengthwise with serrated knife; scoop out flesh into large bowl. Reserve skins. Add three fourths buttermilk mixture, ½ teaspoon salt and three fourths onions to bowl. Mash with potato masher until smooth.

5 Cut sweet potatoes in half lengthwise with serrated knife; scoop out flesh into medium bowl. Discard skins. Add remaining one fourth buttermilk mixture, ¼ teaspoon salt and one fourth onions to sweet potatoes. Mash with potato masher until smooth.

6 Fill half of each reserved potato skin horizontally, vertically or diagonally with baked potato mixture; fill other half with sweet potato mixture. Top each stuffed potato half with bacon slice. Transfer stuffed potatoes to baking sheet; bake 15 minutes or until heated through.

GARDEN VEGETABLE PASTA SALAD WITH BACON

MAKES 6 TO 8 SERVINGS

12 ounces uncooked rotini pasta

2 cups broccoli florets

1 can (about 14 ounces) diced tomatoes

2 medium carrots, diagonally sliced

2 stalks celery, sliced

10 medium mushrooms, thinly sliced

½ medium red onion, thinly sliced

½ pound bacon, crisp-cooked and crumbled

1 bottle (8 ounces) Italian or ranch salad dressing

½ cup (2 ounces) shredded Cheddar cheese

1 tablespoon dried parsley flakes

2 teaspoons dried basil

¼ teaspoon black pepper

1 Cook pasta according to package directions. Drain and rinse well under cold water until cool.

2 Combine broccoli, tomatoes, carrots, celery, mushrooms and onion in large bowl. Add pasta and bacon; toss lightly.

3 Add salad dressing, cheese, parsley, basil and pepper; stir to combine.

SERVING SUGGESTION

Serve with French bread and cantaloupe wedges topped with fruit-flavored yogurt.

SKILLET MAC + CHEESE

MAKES 6 SERVINGS

1 pound uncooked cavatappi or rotini pasta

8 ounces thick-cut bacon, cut into ½-inch pieces

¼ cup finely chopped onion

¼ cup all-purpose flour

3½ cups whole milk

1 cup (4 ounces) shredded white Cheddar cheese

1 cup (4 ounces) shredded fontina cheese

1 cup (4 ounces) shredded Gruyère cheese

¾ cup grated Parmesan cheese, divided

½ teaspoon salt

½ teaspoon dry mustard

¼ teaspoon ground red pepper

¼ teaspoon black pepper

¼ cup panko bread crumbs

1 Preheat oven to 400°F. Cook pasta in large saucepan according to package directions until al dente; drain.

2 Meanwhile, cook bacon in large (10-inch) cast iron skillet until crisp; drain on paper towels. Pour drippings into glass measuring cup, leaving thin coating on surface of skillet.

3 Heat 4 tablespoons drippings in large saucepan over medium-high heat. Add onion; cook and stir about 4 minutes or until translucent. Add flour; cook and stir 5 minutes. Slowly add milk over medium-low heat, stirring constantly. Stir in Cheddar, fontina, Gruyère, ½ cup Parmesan, salt, mustard, red pepper and black pepper until smooth and well blended. Add cooked pasta; stir gently until coated. Stir in bacon. Spread mixture in cast iron skillet.

4 Combine panko and remaining ¼ cup Parmesan in small bowl; sprinkle over pasta. Bake 30 minutes or until top is golden brown.

MOUTH-WATERING MAIN DISHES

BACON + TOMATO MELTS

MAKES 4 SANDWICHES

8 slices bacon, crisp-cooked

8 slices (1 ounce each) Cheddar cheese

2 tomatoes, sliced

8 slices whole wheat bread

¼ cup (½ stick) butter, melted

1 Layer 2 slices bacon, 2 slices cheese and tomato slices on each of 2 bread slices; top with remaining bread slices. Brush sandwiches with butter.

2 Heat grill pan or large skillet over medium heat. Add sandwiches; press lightly with spatula or weigh down with small plate. Cook 4 to 5 minutes per side or until cheese melts and sandwiches are golden brown.

MIXED GRILL KABOBS

MAKES 6 TO 8 SERVINGS

1 pound boneless beef sirloin, cut into 1-inch cubes

2 large red, orange or yellow bell peppers, cut into chunks

12 strips bacon, blanched*

12 ounces smoked sausage or kielbasa, cut into ½-inch slices

1 cup peeled red pearl onions or red onion chunks

1 pound pork tenderloin, cut lengthwise in half, then into ¼-inch wide long strips**

1 cup pineapple wedges

1½ cups *Cattlemen's*® Award Winning Classic Barbecue Sauce

To blanch bacon, place bacon strips into boiling water for 1 minute. Drain thoroughly.

You may substitute **Cattlemen's® Authentic Smoke House or Golden Honey Barbecue Sauce.*

1 Arrange beef cubes and 1 bell pepper on metal skewers, weaving bacon strips around all. Place sausage, 1 pepper and onions on separate skewers. Ribbon strips of pork on additional skewers with pineapple wedges.

2 Baste the different kabobs with some of the barbecue sauce. Cook on a well-greased grill over medium-high direct heat, basting often with remaining barbecue sauce.

3 Serve a trio of kabobs to each person with additional sauce.

TIP

To easily cut pork, freeze about 30 minutes until very firm.

GRILLED CHICKEN SANDWICHES WITH BASIL SPREAD WITH REAL MAYONNAISE

MAKES 4 SERVINGS

- ⅓ cup HELLMANN'S® or BEST FOODS® Real Mayonnaise
- ¼ cup finely chopped fresh basil leaves
- ¼ cup grated Parmesan cheese
- 8 slices whole-grain bread
- 1 pound boneless, skinless chicken breast halves, grilled and sliced
- 4 slices bacon, crisp-cooked and halved crosswise

Combine HELLMANN'S® or BEST FOODS® Real Mayonnaise, basil and cheese in small bowl. Evenly spread mixture on bread slices. Equally top 4 bread slices with chicken and bacon, then top with remaining bread slices.

PEANUT BUTTER BLT WRAPS

MAKES 4 SERVINGS

- ½ cup SKIPPY® Creamy, SUPER CHUNK® or Roasted Honey Nut Peanut Butter
- 4 (6-inch) fajita-size flour tortillas
- 8 slices bacon, crisp-cooked
- 4 lettuce leaves
- 1 large tomato, sliced

Evenly spread SKIPPY® Creamy Peanut Butter over tortillas, then evenly top with remaining ingredients; roll up. To serve, cut each wrap in half.

NOTE

A portable lunch that travels well.
Experiment with different flavor tortillas.

BAKED CHICKEN WITH BACON-TOMATO SAUCE

MAKES 4 SERVINGS

2 cups canned fire-roasted diced tomatoes*

4 pounds bone-in chicken pieces (about 8 pieces)

¾ teaspoon salt, divided

¼ teaspoon black pepper

Nonstick cooking spray

6 slices bacon, cut into 1-inch pieces

1 onion, cut into ½-inch pieces

Fire-roasted tomatoes give this dish a deeper, more complex flavor. Look for them in your supermarket or specialty store next to the other canned tomato products.

1 Preheat oven to 450°F. Spread tomatoes on bottom of 13×9-inch baking dish.

2 Season chicken with ½ teaspoon salt and pepper. Spray large skillet with cooking spray; heat over medium-high heat. Add chicken; cook 8 minutes or until browned and crisp, turning once. Transfer to baking dish. Bake 30 to 40 minutes or until chicken is cooked through (165°F).

3 Meanwhile, cook bacon in same skillet over medium-high heat about 8 minutes or until crisp, turning once. Drain on paper towels. Reserve drippings in skillet.

4 Cook onion in drippings 8 minutes or until golden, stirring occasionally. Drain fat. Stir in remaining ¼ teaspoon salt.

5 Serve chicken with tomatoes, bacon and onions.

TOASTED COBB SALAD SANDWICHES

MAKES 2 SANDWICHES

½ medium avocado

1 green onion, chopped

½ teaspoon lemon juice

Salt and black pepper

2 Kaiser rolls, split

4 ounces thinly sliced deli chicken or turkey

4 slices bacon, crisp-cooked

1 hard-cooked egg, sliced

2 slices (1 ounce each) Cheddar cheese

½ cup crumbled blue cheese

Tomato slices (optional)

Olive oil

1 Mash avocado in small bowl; stir in green onion and lemon juice. Season with salt and pepper. Spread avocado mixture on cut sides of roll tops.

2 Layer bottoms of rolls with chicken, bacon, egg, Cheddar cheese, blue cheese and tomato, if desired. Close sandwiches with roll tops. Brush outsides of sandwiches lightly with oil.

3 Heat large nonstick skillet over medium heat. Add sandwiches; cook 4 to 5 minutes per side or until cheese is melted and sandwiches are golden brown.

FETTUCCINE ALLA CARBONARA

MAKES 4 SERVINGS

12 ounces uncooked fettuccine

4 ounces bacon, cut crosswise into ½-inch pieces

3 cloves garlic, cut into halves

¼ cup dry white wine

⅓ cup whipping cream

1 egg

1 egg yolk

⅔ cup grated Parmesan cheese, divided

Dash white pepper

1 Cook fettuccine according to package directions. Drain; cover and keep warm.

2 Cook and stir bacon and garlic in large skillet over medium-low heat 4 minutes or until lightly browned. Drain and discard all but 2 tablespoons drippings from skillet.

3 Add wine to skillet; cook over medium heat 3 minutes or until wine is almost evaporated. Add cream; cook and stir 2 minutes. Remove from heat; discard garlic.

4 Whisk egg and egg yolk in top of double boiler; place over simmering water, adjusting heat to maintain simmer. Whisk ⅓ cup cheese and pepper into egg mixture; cook and stir until thickened.

5 Pour bacon mixture over fettuccine; toss to coat. Cook over medium-low heat until heated through. Add egg mixture; toss to coat. Serve with remaining ⅓ cup cheese.

GOURMET BURGERS WITH BACON + GORGONZOLA

MAKES 4 SERVINGS

1½ pounds ground beef

1 cup gorgonzola or blue cheese crumbles

2 tablespoons mayonnaise

4 to 8 slices bacon, crisp-cooked

1 red bell pepper, quartered

4 thick slices red onion

Salt and black pepper

4 egg or brioche rolls, split and toasted

Oak leaf or baby romaine lettuce

1 Prepare grill for direct cooking. Shape beef into four patties about ¾ inch thick. Cover and refrigerate. Combine cheese and mayonnaise in small bowl; refrigerate until ready to serve.

2 Grill bell pepper and onion, covered, over medium-high heat 8 to 10 minutes or until browned, turning once. (Use grill basket, if desired.) Transfer to plate; keep warm.

3 Place patties on grid over medium heat. Grill, covered, 8 to 10 minutes (or uncovered, 13 to 15 minutes) to medium (160°F) or to desired doneness, turning occasionally. Season with salt and black pepper.

4 Spread cheese mixture on cut surfaces of rolls. Top bottom half of each roll with lettuce, burger, bacon, onion, bell pepper and top half of roll.

BACON + ONION BRISKET

MAKES 6 SERVINGS

6 slices bacon, cut crosswise into ½-inch strips

1 flat-cut boneless beef brisket, seasoned with salt and black pepper (about 2½ pounds)

3 medium onions, sliced

2 cans (10½ ounces each) condensed beef broth, undiluted

Salt and black pepper

SLOW COOKER DIRECTIONS

1 Cook bacon in large skillet over medium-high heat about 3 minutes. *Do not overcook.* Transfer bacon with slotted spoon to 5-quart slow cooker.

2 Sear brisket in hot bacon fat on all sides, turning as it browns. Transfer to slow cooker.

3 Reduce skillet heat to medium. Add sliced onions to skillet; cook and stir 3 to 5 minutes or until softened. Add to slow cooker. Pour in broth. Cover; cook on HIGH 6 to 8 hours.

4 Transfer brisket to large cutting board; let rest 10 minutes. Slice brisket against the grain into thin slices, and arrange on platter. Season with salt and pepper. Spoon bacon, onions and cooking liquid over brisket to serve.

BACON, LETTUCE + SALSA WRAPS

MAKES 12 WRAPS

10 slices bacon

12 (8-inch) ORTEGA® Flour Soft Tortillas

 1 cup ORTEGA® Salsa, any variety

¼ cup mayonnaise

½ head iceberg lettuce, shredded

FRY bacon according to package directions until just done. Drain well on paper towel. Chop into small pieces.

WRAP tortillas with clean, lightly moistened cloth or paper towels. Microwave on HIGH (100% power) 1 minute, or until hot and pliable.

COMBINE salsa and mayonnaise in small bowl. Spread generously on tortillas. Divide bacon evenly among tortillas, placing down center of tortilla. Sprinkle evenly with shredded lettuce. Fold ends of tortilla to middle, then roll tightly around mixture. Cut diagonally to serve.

TIP

For added flavor, include shredded Cheddar cheese in the wraps.

MACARONI + CHEESE WITH BACON

MAKES 4 SERVINGS

8 ounces uncooked rotini pasta

2 tablespoons butter

2 tablespoons all-purpose flour

¼ teaspoon salt

¼ teaspoon dry mustard

⅛ teaspoon black pepper

1½ cups milk

2 cups (8 ounces) shredded sharp Cheddar cheese

12 slices bacon, crisp-cooked and crumbled

2 medium tomatoes, sliced

1 Preheat oven to 350°F. Lightly grease shallow 1½-quart casserole.

2 Cook pasta according to package directions; drain and return to saucepan.

3 Melt butter in medium saucepan over medium-low heat. Whisk in flour, salt, mustard and pepper; cook and stir 1 minute. Whisk in milk. Bring to a boil over medium heat, stirring frequently. Reduce heat to low. Simmer 2 minutes. Remove from heat. Add cheese; stir until melted. Add cheese mixture and bacon to pasta; stir until well blended. Transfer to prepared casserole.

4 Bake, uncovered, 20 minutes. Arrange tomato slices on casserole. Bake 5 to 8 minutes or until hot and bubbly.

GYPSY'S BBQ CHICKEN

MAKES 6 SERVINGS

6 boneless skinless chicken breasts (about 1½ pounds)

1 bottle (26 ounces) barbecue sauce

6 slices bacon

6 slices Swiss cheese

SLOW COOKER DIRECTIONS

1 Place chicken in slow cooker. Cover with barbecue sauce. Cover; cook on LOW 8 to 9 hours.

2 Before serving, cut bacon slices in half. Cook bacon in microwave or on stove top, keeping bacon flat.

3 Place 2 slices cooked bacon over each piece of chicken in slow cooker. Top with cheese slices. Turn slow cooker to HIGH. Cover; cook on HIGH 5 to 10 minutes or until cheese is melted.

NOTE

If sauce becomes too thick during cooking, add a little water.

SALSA BACON BURGERS WITH GUACAMOLE

MAKES 4 BURGERS

- 1 pound ground beef
- 1 packet (1.25 ounces) ORTEGA® Taco Seasoning Mix
- ¼ cup ORTEGA® Salsa, any variety
- 2 ripe avocados
- 1 packet (1 ounce) ORTEGA® Guacamole Seasoning Mix
- 4 hamburger buns
- 8 slices cooked bacon

COMBINE ground beef, taco seasoning mix and salsa in large mixing bowl. With clean hands, form meat mixture into 4 patties.

CUT avocados in half and remove pits. Scoop out avocado meat and smash in small bowl. Add guacamole seasoning mix. Set aside.

HEAT large skillet over medium heat; cook burgers 5 minutes. Flip burgers and continue to cook another 7 minutes.

PLACE burgers on bottom of buns. Top each burger with dollop of guacamole, 2 slices bacon and top bun.

BACON + CHEESE RAREBIT

MAKES 6 SERVINGS

1½ tablespoons butter

½ cup lager (not dark beer)

2 teaspoons Worcestershire sauce

2 teaspoons Dijon mustard

⅛ teaspoon ground red pepper

2 cups (8 ounces) shredded American cheese

1½ cups (6 ounces) shredded sharp Cheddar cheese

1 small loaf (8 ounces) egg bread or challah, cut into 6 (1-inch-thick) slices

12 large slices tomato

12 slices bacon, crisp-cooked

1 Preheat broiler. Line medium baking sheet with foil.

2 Melt butter in double boiler set over simmering water. Stir in lager, Worcestershire sauce, mustard and red pepper; cook until heated through, stirring occasionally. Gradually add cheeses, stirring constantly until melted. Remove from heat; cover and keep warm.

3 Broil bread slices until golden brown. Arrange on prepared baking sheet. Top each serving with tomato and bacon. Spoon about ¼ cup cheese sauce evenly over each serving. Broil 4 to 5 inches from heat just until cheese sauce begins to brown.

SWEET + SAVORY TREATS

CARAMEL BACON NUT BROWNIES

MAKES 2 DOZEN BROWNIES

¾ cup (1½ sticks) butter

4 squares (1 ounce each) unsweetened chocolate

2 cups sugar

4 eggs

1 cup all-purpose flour

1 package (14 ounces) caramels

¼ cup whipping cream

2 cups coarsely chopped pecans, divided

4 slices bacon, crisp-cooked and crumbled

1 package (12 ounces) chocolate chunks or chips,
   divided

1 Preheat oven to 350°F. Grease 13×9-inch baking pan.

2 Place butter and chocolate in large microwavable bowl.
Microwave on HIGH 1½ to 2 minutes or until melted and
smooth. Stir in sugar. Add eggs, one at a time, beating
until blended after each addition. Stir in flour. Spread half
of batter in prepared pan. Bake 20 minutes.

3 Meanwhile, combine caramels and cream in medium
microwavable bowl. Microwave on HIGH 1½ to 2 minutes or
until caramels begin to melt; stir until smooth. Stir in 1 cup
pecans and bacon.

4 Spread caramel mixture over partially baked brownie
layer. Sprinkle with half of chocolate chunks. Pour
remaining brownie batter over top; sprinkle with
remaining 1 cup pecans and chocolate chunks. Bake
25 minutes or until set. Cool completely in pan on wire
rack. Cut into squares.

BACON-CHEDDAR MUFFINS

MAKES 12 MUFFINS

2 cups all-purpose flour

¾ cup sugar

2 teaspoons baking powder

½ teaspoon baking soda

½ teaspoon salt

¾ cup plus 2 tablespoons milk

⅓ cup butter, melted and cooled

1 egg

1 cup (4 ounces) shredded Cheddar cheese

6 slices bacon, crisp-cooked and crumbled

1 Preheat oven to 350°F. Grease 12 standard (2½-inch) muffin cups or line with paper baking cups.

2 Combine flour, sugar, baking powder, baking soda and salt in medium bowl. Combine milk, butter and egg in small bowl; mix well. Add milk mixture to flour mixture; stir until blended. Gently stir in cheese and bacon. Spoon batter into prepared muffin cups, filling three-fourths full.

3 Bake 15 to 20 minutes or until toothpick inserted into centers comes out clean. Cool in pan 2 minutes; remove to wire rack.

CHOCOLATE-COVERED BACON

MAKES 12 SLICES

12 slices thick-cut bacon

12 wooden skewers (12 inches)

1 cup semisweet chocolate chips

1 cup white chocolate chips or butterscotch chips

2 tablespoons shortening, divided

1 Thread each bacon slice onto a wooden skewer. Place on a rack in large baking pan. Bake at 400°F 20 to 25 minutes or until crisp. Cool completely.

2 Combine semisweet chocolate chips and 1 tablespoon shortening in large microwavable bowl. Microwave on HIGH 30 seconds; stir until smooth.

3 Combine white chocolate chips and remaining 1 tablespoon shortening in large microwavable bowl. Continue to microwave on HIGH at 30-second intervals until melted and smooth.

4 Drizzle chocolates over each bacon slice as desired. Place on waxed paper-lined baking sheets. Refrigerate until firm. Store in refrigerator.

BEER, CARAMELIZED ONION, BACON + PARMESAN MUFFINS

MAKES 12 SERVINGS

- 6 slices bacon, chopped
- 2 cups chopped onions
- 3 teaspoons sugar, divided
- ¼ teaspoon dried thyme
- 1½ cups all-purpose flour
- ¾ cup grated Parmesan cheese
- 2 teaspoons baking powder
- ½ teaspoon salt
- ¾ cup lager or other light-colored beer
- 2 eggs
- ¼ cup extra virgin olive oil

1 Preheat oven to 375°F. Grease 12 standard (2½-inch) muffin cups.

2 Cook bacon in large skillet over medium heat until crisp, stirring occasionally. Drain on paper towel-lined plate. Add onions, 1 teaspoon sugar and thyme to skillet; cook 12 minutes or until onions are golden brown, stirring occasionally. Cool 5 minutes; stir in bacon.

3 Combine flour, cheese, baking powder, salt and remaining 2 teaspoons sugar in large bowl. Whisk lager, eggs and oil in medium bowl. Add to flour mixture; stir just until dry ingredients are moistened. Gently stir in onion mixture. Spoon batter evenly into prepared muffin cups.

4 Bake 15 minutes or until toothpick inserted into centers comes out clean. Cool in pan 5 minutes; remove to wire rack. Serve warm.

CHOCOLATE MAPLE BUNDT CAKE WITH BACON

MAKES 16 SERVINGS

1 package (about 18 ounces) chocolate cake mix

1 package (4-serving size) chocolate instant pudding mix

4 eggs, beaten

¾ cup water

¾ cup sour cream

½ cup bacon grease (fat)

6 ounces (1 cup) semisweet chocolate chips

Maple Glaze (recipe follows)

4 slices bacon, crisp-cooked and crumbled

1 Preheat oven to 350°F. Spray 12–cup (10-inch) bundt or tube pan with nonstick cooking spray.

2 Beat cake mix, pudding mix, eggs, water, sour cream and bacon grease in large bowl with electric mixer at medium speed until ingredients are blended. Stir in chocolate chips; pour into prepared pan.

3 Bake 55 to 60 minutes or until cake springs back when lightly touched. Prepare Maple Glaze. Cool cake 1 hour in pan on wire rack. Invert cake onto large serving plate; cool completely. Pour Maple Glaze over cake. Sprinkle with crumbled bacon.

MAPLE GLAZE

2 tablespoons butter, softened

2 tablespoons maple or pancake syrup

1½ cups powdered sugar

2 to 4 tablespoons milk

Beat butter and maple syrup in medium bowl until blended. Gradually beat in powdered sugar and 2 tablespoons milk. Add additional milk, by tablespoon, until desired consistency is reached.

CRUNCHY BACON + CHEESE COOKIES

MAKES ABOUT 4 DOZEN COOKIES

⅔ cup butter, softened

⅔ cup sugar

1 egg

1 teaspoon vanilla

¾ cup all-purpose flour

½ teaspoon baking soda

½ teaspoon salt

1¼ cups old-fashioned oats

1 cup (4 ounces) shredded sharp Cheddar cheese

6 slices bacon, crisp-cooked and crumbled

½ cup honey-nut wheat germ*

Wheat germ is available in most large supermarkets, but a greater variety of brands and flavors is available at most health food stores.

1 Preheat oven to 350°F. Lightly spray cookie sheets with nonstick cooking spray.

2 Beat butter and sugar in large bowl with electric mixer on medium speed until light and fluffy. Add egg and vanilla; beat well. Sift together flour, baking soda and salt in small bowl; gradually add to creamed mixture, beating until well blended. Stir in remaining ingredients.

3 Drop dough by rounded teaspoonfuls 2 inches apart onto prepared cookie sheets. Bake 10 to 12 minutes or until golden brown. Cool slightly on cookie sheets. Remove to wire racks; cool completely.

BACON + TOMATO
DROP BISCUITS

MAKES 10 BISCUITS

¼ cup thinly sliced sun-dried tomatoes (not packed in oil)

1 cup biscuit baking mix

1 tablespoon cold unsalted butter, cut into thin slices

6 to 8 tablespoons milk

1 tablespoon minced fresh chives

⅓ cup cooked chopped bacon

1 Preheat oven to 400°F. Line baking sheet with parchment paper or coat with nonstick cooking spray; set aside. Place tomatoes in heatproof bowl. Cover with very hot water; let stand 10 minutes. Drain well. Chop tomatoes to a pulp.

2 Place biscuit mix in medium bowl. Cut in butter with pastry blender or two knives until mixture resembles coarse crumbs. Add enough milk to make soft sticky dough. Gently knead in tomatoes, chives and bacon. Drop dough by heaping tablespoonfuls 2 inches apart onto prepared baking sheet.

3 Bake 14 to 16 minutes or until golden brown. Transfer to wire rack to cool slightly. Serve warm.

EASY CHEESY BACON BREAD

MAKES 12 SERVINGS

1 pound sliced bacon, chopped

1 onion, chopped

1 green bell pepper, chopped

½ teaspoon ground red pepper

3 packages (7½ ounces each) refrigerated buttermilk biscuits, separated and quartered

2½ cups (10 ounces) shredded Cheddar cheese, divided

½ cup (1 stick) butter, melted

1 Preheat oven to 350°F. Spray bundt pan with nonstick cooking spray.

2 Cook bacon in large skillet over medium heat until crisp. Drain on paper towels. Reserve 1 tablespoon drippings in skillet. Add onion, bell pepper and red pepper; cook and stir over medium-high heat 10 minutes or until tender. Cool.

3 Combine biscuit pieces, bacon, onion mixture, 2 cups cheese and melted butter in large bowl; mix gently. Loosely press mixture into prepared bundt pan.

4 Bake 30 minutes or until golden brown. Cool in pan 5 minutes. Invert onto large serving platter and sprinkle with remaining ½ cup cheese. Serve warm.

BACON S'MORES BUNDLES

MAKES 4 SERVINGS

- 1¼ cups mini marshmallows
- ¾ cup semisweet chocolate chips
- ¾ cup coarsely crushed graham crackers (5 whole graham crackers)
- 4 slices bacon, crisp-cooked and crumbled
- 1 package (about 17 ounces) frozen puff pastry, thawed

1 Preheat oven to 400°F. Combine marshmallows, chocolate chips, graham crackers and bacon in medium bowl.

2 Unfold pastry on lightly floured surface. Roll each pastry sheet into 12-inch square; cut into four 6-inch squares. Place scant ½ cup marshmallow mixture in center of each square.

3 Brush edges of pastry squares with water. Bring edges together over filling; twist tightly to seal. Place bundles 2 inches apart on ungreased baking sheet.

4 Bake 20 minutes or until golden brown. Cool on wire rack 5 minutes; serve warm.

CHOCOLATE CHIP BACON COOKIES

MAKES ABOUT 3 DOZEN COOKIES

1¼ cups all-purpose flour

½ teaspoon salt

½ teaspoon baking soda

½ cup (1 stick) butter, softened

½ cup granulated sugar

¼ cup packed light brown sugar

1 egg, lightly beaten

1 teaspoon vanilla

1 cup semisweet chocolate chips

6 slices bacon, crisp-cooked and crumbled

½ cup coarsely chopped walnuts

1 Preheat oven to 350°F. Lightly grease cookie sheets. Combine flour, salt and baking soda in medium bowl.

2 Beat butter, granulated sugar and brown sugar in large bowl with electric mixer at medium speed until light and fluffy. Add egg and vanilla; beat until well blended. Add flour mixture; beat just until blended. Stir in chocolate chips, bacon and walnuts.

3 Drop tablespoonfuls of dough 2 inches apart onto prepared cookie sheets.

4 Bake 16 to 18 minutes or until edges are lightly browned. Cool on cookie sheets 1 minute. Remove to wire racks; cool completely.

BACON CHEDDAR MONKEY BREAD

MAKES 12 SERVINGS

1¾ cups (7 ounces) shredded sharp Cheddar cheese

12 ounces bacon, cooked and chopped (about 1 cup)

¼ cup finely chopped green onions

2¾ to 3 cups all-purpose flour, divided

1 package (¼ ounce) rapid-rise active dry yeast

1 teaspoon salt

1 cup warm water (120°F)

2 tablespoons olive oil

⅓ cup butter, melted

1 egg

1 Combine cheese, bacon and green onions in medium bowl; mix well.

2 Combine 1½ cups flour, yeast and salt in large bowl; stir to combine. Add water and oil; beat with electric mixer at medium speed 3 minutes.

3 Beat in 1¼ cups flour until dough comes together. Add 1 cup cheese mixture; beat at medium-low speed 6 to 8 minutes or until dough is smooth and elastic, adding remaining ¼ cup flour if necessary to clean side of bowl. Place dough in greased bowl; turn to grease top. Cover; let rise in warm place about 30 minutes or until doubled in size.

4 Generously spray 12-cup (10-inch) bundt pan with nonstick cooking spray. Whisk butter and egg in shallow bowl until blended. Punch down dough. Roll 1-inch pieces of dough into balls. Dip balls in butter mixture; roll in remaining cheese mixture to coat. Layer in prepared pan. Cover; let rise in warm place about 40 minutes or until almost doubled in size. Preheat oven to 375°F.

5 Bake about 35 minutes or until golden brown. Loosen edges of bread with knife; invert onto wire rack. Cool 5 minutes; serve warm.

OLD-FASHIONED CARAMEL + CANDIED BACON APPLES

MAKES 6 APPLES

Candied Bacon (recipe follows), crumbled

1 package (14 ounces) caramels

2 tablespoons water

6 wooden craft sticks

6 medium Granny Smith apples

1 Prepare Candied Bacon.

2 Place caramels and water in medium heavy saucepan. Cook, stirring frequently, over medium-low heat until melted and very hot.

3 Insert stick into stem end of each apple. Place crumbled bacon in shallow bowl. Dip apple into caramel, tilting saucepan until apple is coated; let excess caramel drip back into saucepan. Remove excess caramel by scraping bottom of apple across rim of saucepan.

4 Immediately roll apple in crumbled bacon. Place, stick side up, on large baking sheet lined with waxed paper. Repeat with remaining apples. Rewarm caramel, if needed. Refrigerate at least 10 minutes or until caramel is firm.

CANDIED BACON

4 to 6 slices thick-cut bacon

¼ to ½ cup packed brown sugar

Preheat oven to 400°F. Line 15×10-inch jelly-roll pan with heavy-duty foil. Coat both sides of each strip of bacon with brown sugar. Bake 18 to 20 minutes or until crispy (Bacon should be turned over after 10 minutes).

ACKNOWLEDGMENTS

The publisher would like to thank the companies and organizations listed below for the use of their recipes and photographs in this publication.

ConAgra Foods, Inc.

Dole Food Company, Inc.

The Hershey Company

Ortega®, A Division of B&G Foods, Inc.

Reckitt Benckiser LLC.

Recipes courtesy of the Reynolds Kitchens

Sargento® Foods Inc.

Unilever

Wisconsin Milk Marketing Board

METRIC
CONVERSION CHART

VOLUME MEASUREMENTS (dry)

1/8 teaspoon = 0.5 mL
1/4 teaspoon = 1 mL
1/2 teaspoon = 2 mL
3/4 teaspoon = 4 mL
1 teaspoon = 5 mL
1 tablespoon = 15 mL
2 tablespoons = 30 mL
1/4 cup = 60 mL
1/3 cup = 75 mL
1/2 cup = 125 mL
2/3 cup = 150 mL
3/4 cup = 175 mL
1 cup = 250 mL
2 cups = 1 pint = 500 mL
3 cups = 750 mL
4 cups = 1 quart = 1 L

VOLUME MEASUREMENTS (fluid)

1 fluid ounce (2 tablespoons) = 30 mL
4 fluid ounces (1/2 cup) = 125 mL
8 fluid ounces (1 cup) = 250 mL
12 fluid ounces (1 1/2 cups) = 375 mL
16 fluid ounces (2 cups) = 500 mL

WEIGHTS (mass)

1/2 ounce = 15 g
1 ounce = 30 g
3 ounces = 90 g
4 ounces = 120 g
8 ounces = 225 g
10 ounces = 285 g
12 ounces = 360 g
16 ounces = 1 pound = 450 g

DIMENSIONS

1/16 inch = 2 mm
1/8 inch = 3 mm
1/4 inch = 6 mm
1/2 inch = 1.5 cm
3/4 inch = 2 cm
1 inch = 2.5 cm

OVEN TEMPERATURES

250°F = 120°C
275°F = 140°C
300°F = 150°C
325°F = 160°C
350°F = 180°C
375°F = 190°C
400°F = 200°C
425°F = 220°C
450°F = 230°C

BAKING PAN SIZES

Utensil	Size in Inches/Quarts	Metric Volume	Size in Centimeters
Baking or Cake Pan (square or rectangular)	8×8×2	2 L	20×20×5
	9×9×2	2.5 L	23×23×5
	12×8×2	3 L	30×20×5
	13×9×2	3.5 L	33×23×5
Loaf Pan	8×4×3	1.5 L	20×10×7
	9×5×3	2 L	23×13×7
Round Layer Cake Pan	8×1½	1.2 L	20×4
	9×1½	1.5 L	23×4
Pie Plate	8×1¼	750 mL	20×3
	9×1¼	1 L	23×3
Baking Dish or Casserole	1 quart	1 L	—
	1½ quart	1.5 L	—
	2 quart	2 L	—